**LUFTWAFFE AT WAR**

# Airwar over
# the Atlantic

This Fw 200 C-4 is armed with a single MG 151/20 gun on the fuselage roof and a small movable MG 15 fixed in the forward dorsal turret of the aircraft. The large emblem of KG 40 can be seen on the fuselage. Just off the runway, two patrolling German soldiers appear to be protecting both the aircraft and two cows lying on the grass!

# LUFTWAFFE AT WAR

# Airwar over the Atlantic

Manfred Griehl

Pen & Sword
AVIATION

*Airwar over the Atlantic*

A Greenhill Book
First published in 2003 by Greenhill Books,
Lionel Leventhal Limited
www.greenhillbooks.com

This edition published in 2016 by
PEN & SWORD AVIATION
An imprint of
Pen & Sword Books Ltd
47 Church Street
Barnsley
South Yorkshire
S70 2AS

ISBN: 978-1-84832-791-7

CIP data records for this title are available
from the British Library.

Designed by DAG Publications Ltd
Design by David Gibbons
Layout by Anthony A. Evans

Printed and bound in Malta by Gutenberg Press Ltd

Pen & Sword Books Ltd incorporates the Imprints
of Aviation, Atlas, Family History, Fiction, Maritime,
Military, Discovery, Politics, History, Archaeology,
Select, Wharncliffe Local History, Wharncliffe True
Crime, Military Classics, Wharncliffe Transport,
Leo Cooper, The Praetorian Press, Remember When,
Seaforth Publishing and Frontline Publishing.

For a complete list of Pen & Sword titles
please contact
PEN & SWORD BOOKS LIMITED
47 Church Street, Barnsley, South Yorkshire,
S70 2AS, England
E-mail: enquiries@pen-and-sword.co.uk
Website: www.pen-and-sword.co.uk

# LUFTWAFFE AT WAR
# AIRWAR OVER THE ATLANTIC

In late 1938 the supreme command of the German Navy (*Oberkommando der Kriegsmarine*) began to examine the application of air power to naval operations, although, since the Third Reich confidently expected at this stage to avoid a war with Britain, planning would have been for a worst-case scenario, rather than to meet a specific expectation. Initially therefore the main task of the air units assigned to the *Kriegsmarine* was coastal reconnaissance.

Using improved and better aircraft, including land-based types such as the Ju 88 that exhibited far better performance characteristics than the then current maritime types, more effective methods of maritime warfare were explored. Different plans worked out by the *Oberkommando der Kriegsmarine* attempted to achieve closer aerial co-operation with vessels of the German navy. Air power could, for example, potentially be harnessed to provide timely reconnaissance to allow surface raiders to reach the Atlantic without detection and, if necessary, provide air intervention. It could also be used to provide targets for U-boats, although in the vast expanse of the Atlantic this was often less than useful; it could be used to carry out direct attacks on enemy surface assets; and it could be used in mine laying to inhibit enemy movements. Nevertheless, in early 1940 co-operation with *Kriegsmarine* surface vessels and U-boats was almost non-existent.

Early in WWII, attacks on British ground targets were prohibited by the German Supreme Command. Permission to resume these attacks was finally granted by the German naval staff, following which He 59s were used to lay naval mines in the Downs, Thames Estuary and off Sheerness. After experiencing a number of technical difficulties, the operations then declined. Important targets, such as Liverpool and Belfast, were out of range for the slow He 59. Subsequently, aircrew flying the He 111 carried out mine laying operations.

Operating at night, the aircraft available at this time, such as the He 59 and Do 18, would have been fairly adequate in laying mines in shipping lanes or harbour approaches. However, until the He 115 entered service in late 1939, there were no suitable torpedo bombers and the German air torpedoes then available were not of a suitably reliable standard. Meanwhile magnetic mines, although initially successful, were recovered by the British, enabling them to devise countermeasures against these devices. Despite this, it seemed nevertheless to be possible to attack smaller enemy vessels by day or at dawn. Unfortunately, the inventory of then available twin-engined maritime aircraft of the German *Marineflieger* under the command of the *Führer der Luftstreitkräfte* (the A.O.C.'s Fleet Air Arm) was too short in range to be able to action orders for missions over all the seas bordering Europe.

Additionally, the aircrafts' reconnaissance capabilities did not allow many missions a day due to a limited number of experienced, fully trained crews; also the navigation systems for these kinds of mission were still under development.

The obsolescent twin-engined He 59 floatplanes and reconnaissance aircraft such as the He 60 and the Do 18 flying boat did not seem to be sufficiently powerful to play an important role quickly enough in the modern conflict emerging over the seas of Western Europe.

In 1939 it was suggested that fourteen carrier-borne units be raised, so-called *Trägerstaffeln*, to be used for the sole German aircraft carrier then under development, the *Graf Zeppelin*.

Additionally, a new schedule spoke about establishing not less than fifty units (*Staffeln*) including seven reconnaissance units stationed on big *Kriegsmarine* vessels (so-called *Bordflieger-staffeln*) to be built up by 1942. Of the remaining units, sixteen should belong to the German coastal command structure consisting of sea reconnaissance units equipped with flying boats and float planes, the others being equipped with land-based long-range combat aircraft.

Six offensive units, called *Fernkampfstaffeln* (*Land*) (land-based long-range combat units), were estimated to be sufficient to attack enemy forces all over the North Sea and Baltic Sea over the following few years; in fact these units did achieve some good results.

On 24 November 1938, *Kapitän zur See* Fricke of the German *Seekriegsleitung* (Supreme Command of the Navy) and *Oberst* (Colonel) H.G. Jeschonnek (General Staff of the Luftwaffe) discussed the need for the growth of the Luftwaffe over the coming years. Besides attacking the Soviet Union, both believed that potential future enemies could be France and Great Britain. In order to eliminate the powerful British Navy and destroy merchant ships arming the British Isles, both agreed that some thirteen Luftwaffe *Geschwader* would be needed. A further thirty *Geschwader* should attack harbours, airfields and industrial targets all over England. This projection was in fact optimistic. As of 1940, only fourteen *Kampfgeschwader* were ranged against England, totalling forty-two *Gruppen*, plus nine *Gruppen* of *Stukas* and two coastal *Gruppen*. Because Germany believed that England could be assisted by the USA, it became obvious that well protected convoys would be used to support the besieged British Isles. However, it seems that both German officers thought that it was inevitable that the Luftwaffe would be successful. Only later would it become apparent that there was a great need for long-range land-based combat aircraft operating over both the North Sea and the Atlantic.

One of the units urgently needed was *Kampfgeschwader* (KG) 40. This combat unit was under the command of X. *Fliegerkorps* led by *Generalleutnant* Hans Geisler who had joined the *Kriegsmarine* on 1 April and who had become the *Führer der Luftstreitkräfte* of the *Kriegsmarine* on 1 October 1935. From 3 October 1939 he became responsible for X. *Fliegerkorps*, a position he held until August 1942. Because the tactical range of the Do 17, He 111 and Ju 88 were all poor for the maritime missions he had in mind, *General* Geisler had no opportunity to carry out offensive raids west of England and Ireland. However, the large four-engined Fw 200, a former transport aircraft of *Deutsche Lufthansa,* did offer sufficient range (but rather poor performance) to conduct a maritime air offensive far away from Germany. Besides this aircraft, only the Ju 90, of which only two had been available in 1939, seemed also to represent a step in the right direction.

*Major* Edgar Petersen, the leader of the first *Gruppe* of KG 40, which was established on 1 November 1939 near Bremen, flying the He 111 E, suggested using modified Fw 200s to carry out long-range raids. From this idea, a limited number of Fw 200 B-1s, some constructed for the fleet of *Deutsche Lufthansa,* were subsequently handed over to the Luftwaffe as Fw 200 C-s.

Following attempts to build a Fw 200 for the Imperial Japanese Navy, the Fw 200 V10, an armed long-range version of the aircraft, was constructed. Later, the Fw 200 V11 followed as a prototype for a long-range maritime bomber. From 1 April 1940, the first *Staffel* of KG 40 was the initial unit to receive this new combat aircraft, designated the Fw 200 C-"Condor". Most of the personnel of this *Staffel* were taken from all-weather flying schools all over the Reich. After a few flights, the unit was used for transportation duties between Germany and Norway; taking off from Lüneburg, three Fw 200s of KG 40 headed for Narvik in Norway to support the German mountain soldiers of *General* Dietl. Simultaneously, bombs fell on British vessels on which personnel and material were being brought to Norway and the British positions in that theatre of the war. After the *Wehrmacht* had won the war in Northern Europe, the Fw 200 C "Condors", based at Gardemoen in Norway, flew armed reconnaissance missions over Scotland, the northern isles and over the North Atlantic. On 12 June 1940, after mine laying missions along the British east coast, I./KG 40 was transferred to Bordeaux in France. During the summer of 1940, the crews flew reconnaissance missions up to 24 degrees west. Normally, their long-range aircraft started late in the evening and then headed for Iceland, after that turning south east and later landing at Stavanger or Gardemoen in Norway. After two days of repairs they then moved back to Bordeaux. Because a vast area was controlled from the air, these missions were potentially very useful for the C-in-C of the German submarine service, *Konteradmiral* Karl Dönitz. However, Dönitz's U-boats were usually too distant to be able to act upon any information gathered.

I./KG 40 also had to assist other German forces attacking the city of Liverpool in August 1940 with bombers of *Luftflotten* 2 and 3. After the failure of that mission, *Kampfgruppe* 40 continued with its missions over the Irish Sea, the Northern Channel and the area west of Ireland. Between September 1940 and August 1941, I./KG 40 succeeded in the destruction of many merchant ships on their way from and to the British Isles since most of these ships were unarmed and moved without any protection whatsoever from the Royal Navy.

Up to 31 December 1940, I./KG 40 alone sank more than 800,000 tonnes of civil shipping around England without itself suffering many losses. Over a short period of time, between January and March 1941, nearly ninety merchant vessels with a total tonnage of 390,000 tonnes were claimed to have been destroyed in combat. On 26 October 1940, the 42,000 tonne *Empress of Britain* was set on fire by *Hauptmann* (Captain) Bernhard Jope, belonging to 2./KG 40. Taken in tow, it was torpedoed and sunk two days later by a U-boat. Additionally, *Hauptmann* Fliegel and *Oberleutnant* (First Lieutenant) Buchholz, both later missing in action over the Atlantic, achieved great successes. *Hauptmann* Daser and *Oberleutnant* Verlohr, similarly successful, were decorated with the *Ritterkreuz* (Knight's Cross) for their exploits.

Throughout this period, the "Condor" crews mounted their attacks at very low-level, typically releasing a stick of four SC 250 bombs hundreds of metres from the target ship. Often, one of the bombs would hit the ship's side above, sometimes just below, the waterline. Thus the ship's structure collapsed, breaking apart and sinking immediately, frequently within a few minutes of the initial explosion.

In December 1940, the number of forces being used against maritime targets was enlarged; Kampfgeschwader 40 received a staff unit, the Geschwaderstab, and further operational groups, II.- and III./KG 40 were added.

The main focus of the U-boat and air operations during 1941 and early 1942 lay on the convoy routes from the USA, the South Atlantic and those around Gibraltar. The greatest weight of operations during this time lay with those forces under the command of the Fliegerführer Atlantik, Gustav Harlinghausen. In 1939, Harlinghausen was one of the pioneers of attacking ships with bombs. In the Norwegian campaign he was Chief of Staff of Fliegerkorps X. From March 1943 his anti-shipping forces comprised some 20 "Condors", 24 He 115s and a mixture of Ju 88, Bf 110 and other aircraft used for reconnaissance duties over the sea. Altogether 83 aircraft belonged to Fliegerführer Atlantik at that time. Subsequently, the number of aircraft available for armed reconnaissance missions increased to more than 150, most of them Fw 200s and Ju 88s.

However, from mid-1941, unsustainable losses during low-level attacks forced KG 40 to level bomb from high altitude. These losses were due to the fact that the British Admiralty assembled their merchant ships to form convoys, well escorted by frigates and destroyers of the Royal Navy and Allied maritime powers. Furthermore, the convoys were protected by AA-cruisers and ship-borne barrage balloons to hinder German bomber crews attempting to mount a low-level attack.

Additionally, some of the merchant ships were equipped with Hawker Hurricane fighters mounted on and launched from catapults. On 3 August 1941, the first Fw 200 "Condor" was shot down by a Hurricane pilot who had taken off from such a merchantman.

Despite far better defences, the German flyers were still achieving successes. On 1 March 1941, Major Edgar Petersen took over command of the whole of KG 40. By this time the number of losses had grown steadily. Additionally, from summer 1941 onward, the Royal Navy fielded escort carriers to protect the Allied convoys on all their routes. Due to the increased defensive capability of the enemy forces therefore, the German Führungsstab ordered the Luftwaffe units based in France to fly horizontal attacks from a greater ceiling using the Lotfe 7 bombsight instead of the more common low-level raids. Also, it was suggested to introduce an air-launched torpedo using a limited number of KG 40's bombers to deliver this new weapon, thereby achieving, it was hoped, even greater success in action over the Atlantic. Because the LT F5 torpedo was not very reliable in operation however, all attempts to sink further British ships using it failed.

On 1 September 1941, Major Petersen left KG 40, becoming the new leader of the Erprobungsstelle der Luftwaffe at Rechlin. The new commanding officer of KG 40 was to be Oberst (Colonel) Dr. Pasewaldt.

Since the air defence capability of enlarged Allied convoys grew increasingly effective, German aircrews hoped to receive the more powerful and well protected He 177A as soon as possible. From July 1942, I./KG 40 handed over its remaining Fw 200s to III./KG 40 while Staffel by Staffel, KG 40 received its first He 177As. Due to many technical problems, the operational career of this new, more powerful combat aircraft was rather limited.

The second Gruppe of KG 40 was re-equipped with Do 217 bombers from 1 May 1941 and achieved combat status again in August of that year over the western approaches. Their Staffeln were then sent to Grosseto for aerial torpedo training and exercise duties. In spite of this, II./KG 40 was then placed under the command of Angriffsführer England in March 1943, to be used for level bombing raids over England. In June 1943 the unit was renamed V./KG 2 and left KG 40 entirely. In September 1943, the He 177 A-equipped I./KG 50 was redesignated II./KG 40 at Burg, near Magdeburg, Germany. Assigned to Luftflotte 3, it arrived in Bordeaux on 25 October.

At Bordeaux the crews were trained to operate the rocket-powered Hs 293 A-1 missile, one of which was carried under each wing. Meanwhile, II./KG 100 was using the Do 217 / Hs 293 combination over the Bay of Biscay from August 1943.

After suffering heavy losses during the invasion struggle in June and July 1944, the new second Gruppe was withdrawn to Gardemoen in Norway. The third Gruppe of KG 40 was mainly used over the Mediterranean Sea and operated from various bases in France. After the battle of France was lost the few remaining aircraft of KG 40 were flown to Norway.

In order to intercept Allied convoys headed for Murmansk and Alchelansk in the northern part of Russia, the Luftwaffe operated from newly constructed airfields on the Norwegian-Finnish border. Early in 1942, sixty long-range bombers, thirty dive-bombers and fifteen He 115 floatplanes were based there. However, in spite of bad sailing conditions and several successful attacks, they were unable to stop the convoys from entering Russian waters, and a well prepared AA defence network prevented the Luftwaffe bomber forces from destroying the infrastructure of the two major harbours.

That the German Luftwaffe was unable to sink more ships on their way to Russia was due largely to the convoys' close protection and the number of aircraft used. The convoys also turned as far north as possible, making it difficult for the Luftwaffe to follow them throughout their entire journey. Only the attack mounted against PQ 17 was very successful; more than seventy long-range reconnaissance aircraft (BV 138s, FW 200s and Ju 88s) together with nearly one hundred other combat aircraft (mainly Ju 88 A-4s) and the U-boats of the Kriegsmarine succeeded in destroying several ships.

On 10 July 1944, the *Oberkommando der Luftwaffe* decided to bring I./KG 40 back to full combat strength and to commence delivery of the Me 262 A-1a jet fighter. However, after all attempts to prosecute an offensive air war against the Allies in late 1944 failed, its personnel were dispersed among other units.

The first elements of a fifth *Gruppe* of the then famous *Kampfgeschwader* 40 were established in July 1942 near Bordeaux in France. The crews of a few Ju 88 C-6 *Zerstörer* (destroyer) aircraft became responsible for protecting all German-held areas over the Bay of Biscay against enemy fighters, including well-armed de Havilland Mosquito and Bristol Beaufighter aircraft belonging to the Royal Air Force and British Coastal Command respectively.

From January 1943 the number of these destroyer aircraft available was increasing steadily. This enabled V./KG 40 to fill the lines of three *Staffeln* which operated under the command of *Luftflotte* 3. In August 1943 an additional (fourth) *Staffel* was established, but only a few weeks later this unit left KG 40, their crews being transferred to other destroyer units.

Besides KG 40, *Fernaufklärungsgruppe* (*FAGr.*) 5 assisted German submarine forces by flying reconnaissance missions over the Atlantic Ocean. This unit was commanded by *Major* Fischer and was established on 20 May 1943 after German sinkings of Allied ships had become fewer and fewer. However, more than three units were needed to train and supply the first crews flying the Ju 290 A-3s and A-4s that were used to mount widespread reconnaissance operations over the Atlantic. After a few training missions carried out from Achmer, the aircraft, being fitted with FuG 200 *Hohenthwiel* anti-shipping radar and an increased defensive armament, were sent to Mont de Marsan in France.

In July 1944, *Fernaufklärungsgruppe* 5 was equipped with its largest number of Ju 290s; a total of seventeen aircraft was used in two *Staffeln*, but only eight of them survived to September 1944 when a huge Allied invasion forced the commander of *FAGr.* 5 to withdraw his unit back to the Reich. There the former reconnaissance aircraft were handed over to both KG 200 and *Deutsche Lufthansa*.

During a total of 191 missions, *FAGr.* 5's crews had spent more than 2,438 hours flying over the Atlantic. Their reconnaissance flights covered a distance of 640,750 kilometres, though many of these ende without any enemy contact. Only twenty Allie convoys were found, fourteen with the eyes of Ju 29 aircrew and no more than six with the help of FuG 20 radar installations carried aboard the aircraft. Actin in unison, the German submarines, Fw 200s and H 177s only succeeded in sinking eight destroyers and three (perhaps a few more) merchant vessels; this wa due in large measure to splendid air defensive tactic employed by Allied fighting ships, fighter aircraft and AA-guns mounted on the merchantmen.

The Ju 88 H-1 long-range reconnaissance aircraf played a limited role during the struggle. When it wa first suggested establishing a few units using thi lengthened variant of the Ju 88, only a limited number of ten aircraft (two prototypes [Ju 88 V8 and -V90] and an additional eight series aircraft) had been completed. After the first successful flight of a Ju 88 H-1 *Atlantikaufklärer* (Atlantic reconnaissance aircraft on 2 November 1943, it was proposed to build a series of Ju 88 H-2 *Atlantikzerstörer* (Atlantic destroyer) aircraft, fitted with up to six 20 mm MG 151/20 guns and constructed using parts from the Ju 88 G-4 and Ju 88 S-5 aircraft. Because the fligh characteristics of the H-1 and the H-2 were so different, the complete series was stopped. Of the first H series produced, most were handed over to *Fernaufklärungsgruppe* 123. During May 1944, five o them operated over the Atlantic and the Bay of Biscay to escort German vessels heading for the French coast. However, due to overwhelming air superiority of Allied fighter units, most of the Ju 88 Hs were lost and by September 1944 all Ju 88 Hs had disappeared from the German order of battle.

Several other aircraft had been suggested to continue air reconnaissance duties despite the enemy's strength. Besides the Ar 234, which was designed, amongst other things, to carry out reconnaissance duties over England and the seas around, a radical version of the Do 335, called the Do 635, was tabled by the Supreme Luftwaffe command After development was handed over to Junkers, a conversion based on two joined Do 335 A fuselages was proposed but due to Germany's final defeat in the war only a mock-up was ever finished. Final production of the twin Do 335 failed along with that of another four-engined long-range aircraft, the Me 264. Only a few Ju 188 D-2s fitted with FuG 200 radar were used for further reconnaissance missions, and these only occurred over the North Sea, since the Atlantic Ocean was out of range of German aircraft (flying from Germany, Denmark and Norway) by early 1945. After the production of the Ju 388 was cancelled early in February 1945, a few further missions were carried out by the less powerful Ju 88s, Ju 188s and jet-powered Ar 234 B-2bs. A few remaining aircraft were captured by advancing Allied units up to May 1945 in the northern part of Germany, as well as in Denmark and Norway.

One of the early Fw 200 C-3s after passing a final test flight at Bremen in 1942. The upper forward weapons position was armed with one MG 131 machine gun, the lower position housing a heavy MG FF cannon that was used to keep enemy gunners' heads down during an attack.

**Opposite page:** A last check before this crew board their Fw 200 prior to beginning the next dangerous mission over the Atlantic Ocean during the summer of 1943. The insignia worn on the arms of both officers indicate the rank of *Oberleutnant* (First Lieutenant or Flying Officer).

**Below:** This aircrew belonging to I./KG 40 don their summer flying suits at Bordeaux-Merignac during the summer of 1943. The four-engined aircraft shown in this view, a Fw 200 C of I./KG 40, gives a good impression of the camouflage pattern used by German combat aircraft utilised for maritime operations.

**Opposite page:** The refuelling of a Fw 200 C-3 which was operated by I./KG 40 in France. After refuelling, the aircraft would be transferred to another base or prepared for a maintenance flight since no defensive armament had yet been installed.

**Above:** This close-up view shows the central fin section of a Fw 200 C-1 or C-2 that had taken part in missions flown from Norway over the coastline of Great Britain. The fin markings record one hit scored on an Allied merchantman during an anti-shipping raid or when flying armed reconnaissance.

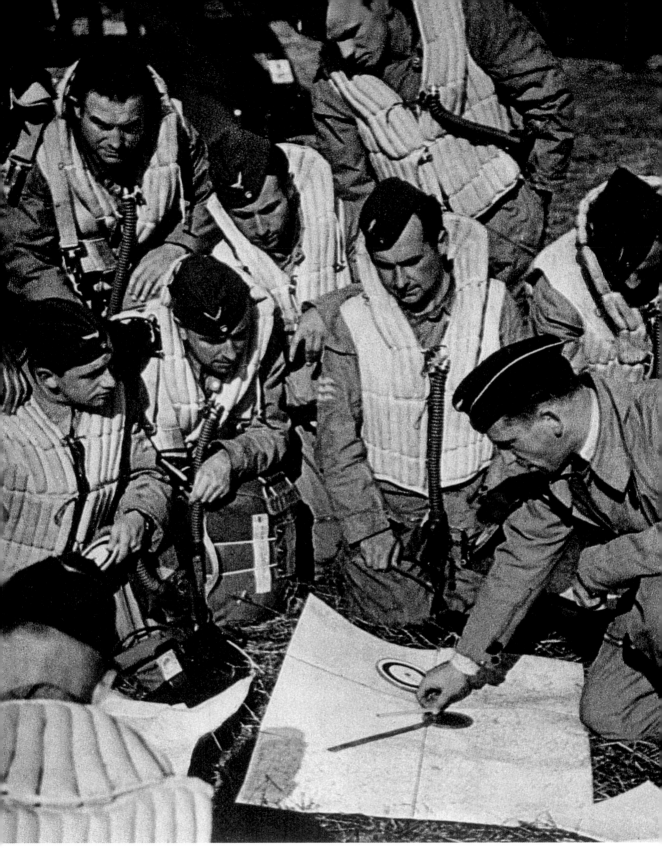

This aircrew is listening intently to instructions from a member of KG 40 staff, describing how to find enemy targets in the vastness of water over which they will shortly be flying. Life jackets were mainly worn by those men operating heavy maritime bombers.

After receiving the necessary mission briefing, aircrews disperse to their Fw 200 C-3 aircraft. This photo shows the early type of camouflage used by combat aircraft operated by the *Staffeln* of KG 40 during missions mounted from the western part of France.

When warming up the four Bramo radial engines, the ground crew would listen out for hidden faults, which, if unremedied, could be disastrous for the crews heading off

**Above:** One of the first Fw 200 C-1s, formerly a B-1 aircraft carrying the production number 0002, primarily designated Fw 200 V11 and used for evaluation purposes. Early in 1940 the aircraft was inspected by *Oberleutnant* Bernhard Jope (left). The photo was taken in front of a huge hangar at Focke-Wulf's works near Bremen. Large plywood drop-tanks (holding 600 litres) could be hung under the outer wings of the aircraft. This aircraft (BS+AG) became flyable on 19 February 1940 and was then handed over to I./KG 40.

**Below:** A close-up view of the *Wega* which was one of the Fw 200 C-1s which belonged to the first *Gruppe* of KG 40, based at Brest airbase in autumn 1940. The first Fw 200 Cs used in offensive action received names such as *Wega*, *Electra* etc. painted on the forward fuselage. The emblem showed the whole world awaiting the attacks of the "Condors".

**Above:** Four Fw 200 C-1 aircraft under construction at Bremen. The forward armament of the early series aircraft consisted of a MG 15 machine gun fitted in a dorsal housing astern of the cockpit and a heavy MG FF installed beneath the fuselage and used for low-level attacks on Allied merchant vessels. The aircraft shown belonged to a series of ten C-1s of which three lack any camouflage due to their early construction.

**Below:** Possibly the first series Fw 200 C-1 in the snowy winter of 1940 at Bremen, prior to one of the evaluation flights conducted by Focke-Wulf crews assisted by personnel of the Luftwaffe. At this stage of development the aircraft were not fitted with guns. In front of the aircraft stands a small fire extinguisher.

**Above:** Bremen, early 1940: after final assembly, the rollout occurs with the help of a number of Focke-Wulf employees. The aircraft was painted in a two-tone green camouflage over all upper surfaces and bright blue over all lower surfaces including all four Bramo 132 radials, which are fitted with three-bladed airscrews. Under the outer wings the fittings for 600 litre drop tanks can be seen.

**Right:** A close-up view of the Fw 200 C-1's Bramo 132 radial engines which provided a maximum performance of 375 km/h, even when flying a fully equipped aircraft. It was able to reach some 450 km/h during a glide attack on ships up to 3,000 metres away and in the case of fog or bad weather could still fly in excess of 230 km/h. The picture was taken before this aircraft was handed over to the Luftwaffe.

**Top:** 1940, after its first evaluation flight, this Fw 200 C-1 was photographed at Bremen airport. In this picture, a complete defensive weapon installation has been fitted. A small MG 15 was installed in a glass housing in the upper B2-position on the rear fuselage, whilst another weapon can be seen in the large bulge under the fuselage where bombs of up to 250 kg each could also be carried.

**Above:** Only low-level attacks on enemy merchant ships were believed to be successful. In the huge bulge beneath the fuselage of this Fw 200 C-1 either a total of twelve SC 50 bombs or up to two SC 500s could be transported under a Schloß 50 or ETC 500 Ixb mount respectively. The picture was taken during an evaluation flight over the North Sea from another factory aircraft in May 1940.

**Opposite page, top:** A close-up view taken during tests of the bomb fittings near both outer radial engines. With the help of a pulley block, large bomb loads such as the SC 250 or SC 500 bombs could be manhandled by ground crew under the wing fittings. The bomb system shown belonged to the Fw 200 C-3. The first of these variants was the Fw 200 V13 (production number 0025), which can be distinguished from other Fw 200 Cs by its increased weapons payload.

**Opposite page, bottom:** This picture shows two heavy bombs fitted under the port outer wing during performance tests. A total of 43 of the Fw 200 C-3 were built, which, due to their larger take-off weight, were powered by four Bramo 323 R-2-radial engines. Over shorter distances it was possible to carry a total of six SC 500 bombs, of which two were housed in the bulge under the middle part of the fuselage.

Opposite page: At the time when Allied convoys were not equipped with sufficient AA guns or air protection using ship-borne barrage balloons, the less armoured Fw 200 became a very low-level attack aircraft. This allowed Oberleutnant Bernhard Jope and his men to sink more than 30,000 tonnes of shipping between August and September 1940. Jope was decorated with the Knights Cross on 30 December 1940 after he had hit the *Empress of Britain* on 26 October 1940, west of Iceland.

Above: A close formation of Fw 200 C-4s crosses the Bay of Biscay awaiting enemy merchant ships. In order to obtain more offensive firepower, both A- and B-positions installed in the forward part of the fuselage were improved by installing two MG 151/20 guns instead of the MG 15 and MG FF. These aircraft were painted in a three-tone camouflage and displayed the KG 40 emblem below the cockpit.

Below: A close-up view of the forward fuselage section of a Fw 200 C-4 combat aircraft belonging to KG 40, which was based in Norway to perform reconnaissance missions over the northern part of the North Sea and the Southern Arctic. At the time the photo was taken the ground crew were removing the canvas protection over the nose section of the aircraft. Note that no weapons were installed when any Fw 200 stood parked on the airfield.

**Left:** Possible defects on the airscrews appear to be hinderin the crew of this KG 4( Fw 200 C from starting their mission over the Atlantic. In order to improve the maintenance capability of the Luftwaffe *Feldwerft* (field maintenance unit) attached to each *Gruppe* of a *Kampfgeschwader*, engine and wireless operations specialists were sent to all major front line units in order to fix technical problems.

**Below:** This aircraft, KE+IK, was a C-3/U4 variant of the Fw 200 and was flown by the crew of *Oberleutnant* Hans Hase. The production number 0086 received the tactical code F8+IH, which indicated that the aircraft belonged to the first *Staffel* of I./KG 30. On 19 December 1941, the entire crew was lost during a long-range reconnaissance mission off the shores of Portugal. The photo shows the aircraft standing on a *Kompensierscheibe*, used in order to help calibrate the master compass installed in the aircraft.

**Above:** These SC 500 bombs are being prepared for action from a "Condor" aircraft by the aircraft's ground crew. With the help of hydraulic trolleys, it was possible to move heavy military loads under the outer wing positions of the Fw 200 C using only a small number of ground crew. Some of the bombs' transportation protection can be seen nearby.

**Below:** This SC 500 bomb is being pulled on its trolley to the main bomb bay of a Fw 200 C-3, this one being named *Mars*. The weathered camouflage indicates that this aircraft had survived many missions up until 1942. In the lower forward weapon position either a single MG FF or, later, a MG 151/20 with better performance could be installed.

**Above:** During the early period of attacks against convoys, German crews often reported no noteworthy defensive action by Allied vessels. However, with time more and more AA guns were fixed on all merchantmen. Furthermore the Royal Navy received more escort destroyers from the USA to provide far better protection against attacking "Condors". Additionally CAM ships (ships equipped with catapults using modified 'Hurricanes' to protect convoys against Fw 200 bombers), and ship-borne barrage balloons were used to deter as many four-engined aircraft as possible from mounting a low-level attack.

**Below:** Fw 200 Cs frequently returned to their bases in France having been damaged in action. A few crews succeeded in reaching French shores with only a few drops of fuel left in their tanks, caused either by bad weather or enemy anti-aircraft hits. Others crashed when their pilots tried to land their damaged "Condors" without working hydraulics or inoperative landing gear. With the help of a captured British crane this Fw 200 C-3 is being recovered and dismantled.

**Above:** After returning to their French bases, all "Condors" of *Kampfgeschwader* 40 were checked immediately by their ground crews. To allow for better inspection of the air crafts' radial engines, stepladders were a common feature in the inventory of the so-called "Black Men" (maintenance crews). Because the Fw 200 C-3 and C-4 did not have sufficient armour protection, even small areas of damage could cause the loss of an aircraft and its crew. Only occasionally would a ditched crew be recovered successfully by one of their own flying boats.

**Below:** There was only a limited maintenance capacity in the Fw 200s' hangars in France, these being used mainly for intensive checkups of the radial engines on which depended a successful return to operations. Some equipment was taken from the former French Air Force or *Air France*, as can be seen on the stepladder under the outer radial engine to the right of the picture.

**Left:** Effort from the whole ground crew was necessary to pull a bomb like a SC 250 onto the modified mounting for cylindrical bomb loads. This picture, taken at Bordeaux in 1942, shows a Fw 200 C-3 belonging to KG 40. The lower rear weapon position normally was fitted with a single MG 15, but in 1942 the position's armament was upgraded by the use of a more powerful MG 131 machine gun.

**Right:** The Fw 200 C-3 and C-4 operated frequently in a formation of two or three aircraft. Thus it was possible that at least one other combat aircraft could report back to the *Kampfgeschwader* if another aircraft was hit or shot down in action. In a few cases, a surviving aircraft crew would drop a rubber dingy and/or other emergency equipment over a downed crew after any enemy convoy had moved out of range.

**Right:** In this picture, only two ground crew members have been necessary to position this SC 250 bomb under one of two PVC 1006 L-positions fitted near the outer engine nacelles under each wing. Alternatively, it was possible to load additional fuel to increase the aircraft's range to a maximum of some 4,500 km., the large 600 litre drop tanks to do this being mounted on a similar underwing position of the Fw 200 C-1.

**Above and below:** Shot down over the wide Atlantic Ocean near a large convoy that this Fw 200 had attacked only a few moments before, the crew leave the aircraft to try to save their own lives. They may have been rescued by one of the ships of the Allied convoy or been found later by a German flying boat. Since the fuel in the main tanks in the middle of the fuselage was largely empty, the aircraft managed to float long enough to allow the crew to leave their bomber and enter the dinghies fixed along the fuselage.

**Above:** Two Fw 200 C-4s in formation during a low-level attack. Because the target aircraft was large enough and due to their weak defences, the Allied AA-gunners succeeded in shooting down or hitting quite a few Fw 200s. One of them was the Fw 200 C-4 of *Oberleutnant* Greul, who operated the same type as shown. On 2 September 1943, *Oblt.* Greul was lost along with his commanding officer, *Leutnant* Händel, a total of five men failing to return.

**Below:** Taken at Bordeaux-Merignac, this photo shows an *Ersteer Wart*, the member of the ground crew who was mainly responsible for the maintenance of his aircraft. In front of the aircraft stands an aircraft fuel tank trailer (*Flugbetriebsstoff-Kesselwagen*, or *Fb.K Anh. 454* for short), which was used on nearly all German air bases in Europe until early 1945.

**Left:** This four-engine bomber is ready for take off. The engines would be tested one last time before the aircraft moved forward to its take off position. This picture was taken in 1942 when an overhauled Fw 200 C-4 had been transferred from Bremen to I. Gruppe of KG 40 at Bordeaux. Compared with other maritime variants of the Fw 200 the engine nacelles feature camouflage used during the middle part of the war.

**Below:** A close-up photo showing the heavy (but moveable) 20 mm MG FF aircraft gun that was fixed in the nose section of the "Condor". First tests using this weapon had been carried out with the first Fw 200 C-1 (V11). Because the MG 151/20 weapon (which had the same calibre) was more effective against ground targets, the first series aircraft were altered to accommodate this better offensive weapon.

**Above:** This Luftwaffe *Oberfeldwebel* belongs to the group of skilled technicians who were responsible for the maintenance of all of the aircraft's armaments. This NCO stands in the aft dorsal position that was equipped with a light MG 15 machine gun firing to the rear. Following the use of escort carriers and CAM ships in Allied convoys, the defensive armament of the type was improved.

**Below:** On operational missions, air gunners wore a flight suit such as this, incorporating an unlined summer flying helmet. In the case of an emergency, possibly when the aircraft was floating on the surface of the water, the crew could leave their aircraft from this position without great problems. Later this gun position was modified to a closed variant.

**Left:** A full crew complement of a Fw 200 C-4 "Condor" on parade. With the exception of the officer standing on the left hand side, all other crewmembers appear to be NCOs or enlisted men. This crew are wearing summer flying dress without life jackets and personal weapons since it is probable that no missions were anticipated over the next few hours.

**Below:** After the Fw 200 C-3 "Condor" had received the more powerful Bramo 323 R-2 radial engines, it was preferable to use a crew of six instead of five men during long missions over the Atlantic. This is a typical photo shot by a member of propaganda unit for the German aviation magazine *Der Adler* (The Eagle), which told its readers about the great successes of the Luftwaffe in all war theatres.

**Above:** This photo shows the use of a 600-litre drop tank during performance tests of a long-range reconnaissance variant in 1942. It is possible that the photo was taken on a base near the French coast. Only a MG 15 is fitted in the lower defensive position rather than the heavy 20 mm weapon, since perhaps no offensive tasks were planned during the mission.

**Below:** A close formation of Fw 200 C-4s over the clouds, crossing the Bay of Biscay on their way to the area over which reconnaissance duties were to be conducted. The leftmost aircraft, F8+CS, belonged to the third *Gruppe* of KG 40 and crashed in France when returning from a mission on 9 November 1943 due to a shortage of fuel.

**Above:** The *Wega*, a Fw 200 C-2, was part of I./KG 40 based in France. Before its first operation over the Atlantic, a combat aircraft was given the name of a star or constellation. In the foreground a former civilian fuel truck is being used for refuelling the aircraft while a specialist works on the forward canopy.

**Left:** This picture was taken during maintenance in Bordeaux. The ground crew can be seen filling the oxygen system of the aircraft using a large iron bottle on wheels. In later variants, the oxygen bottles inside the aircraft were installed behind the B-weapon position. Both aircraft shown are the Fw 200 C-3 variant with one MG 131-turret (A-position) installed on the upper fuselage to the rear of the cockpit. In the D-position a MG 151 was fitted for anti-shipping raids.

**Above:** After the French army had surrendered, several French trucks were taken over by the Luftwaffe and were used by flying units. This Renault is being used to bring an oxygen canister to F8+CR, an aircraft whose camouflage has been partly faded due to many missions over the sea.

**Right:** This veteran aircraft of I./KG 40 had survived many combat missions with a crew commanded by *Oberleutnant* Rose and *Leutnant* von Körber. Besides thirteen attacks against England, the aircraft and its crew had undertaken several missions over the sea and had succeeded in achieving ten hits on British merchantmen.

**Above:** This Fw 200 C-2 was photographed at Bordeaux in 1941. Markings on the fin indicate missions flown over British targets and two hits on merchant ships. A group of ground crew are seen relaxing in the sun together with a civilian specialist sent by the manufacturer.

**Below:** This photo shows F8+CH standing in its well-armoured revetment at Bordeaux-Merignac in the summer of 1942 and being maintained by its ground crew. The walls are filled with earth to give protection to the aircraft of KG 40 in the case of enemy low-level attacks and bomb raids. On the fin of the Fw 200 C-3 (production number 0072) can be seen two ship markings and some other successes marked below the swastika.

**Above:** This photo shows a side view of F8+LS, a Fw 200 C-4 variant, which was operated by 8./KG 40. The C-4 belonged to the most important series of the "Condor", more than ninety aircraft of this type having been manufactured. Only a total of 53 of the following series (C-5 to C-8) were built, quite a few of these by using rebuilt former C-3 and C-4 aircraft.

**Below:** After twenty missions flown over the North Sea, the Bay of Biscay and the Atlantic Ocean, this Fw 200 C shows light damage after returning from a long-range mission. After lifting the rear part of the fuselage, the aircraft was brought to the *Feldwerft* to be repaired quickly since only minor damage had been reported.

**Left:** During take-off for its next mission, this Fw 200 C-3 passes the take-off guard who allowed an aircraft to fly when capable of doing so. Additionally, these men were equipped with fire extinguishers to minimise damage caused by engine fires after testing the Bramo 323 R engines for one last time. Behind the trolley sits a captured French car used by *Kampfgeschwader* 40. The flag indicates the presence of men on the airfield.

**Below:** In order to maximise the chance of finding enemy convoys, a number of Fw 200 Cs, mainly C-4s, were fitted with the *Rostock* radar installation. These were changed shortly afterwards to an improved system, the FuG 200 *Hohenthwiel*, which enabled attacks from a greater range against enemy convoys. Despite all this equipment, only a few radar-assisted attacks actually succeeded.

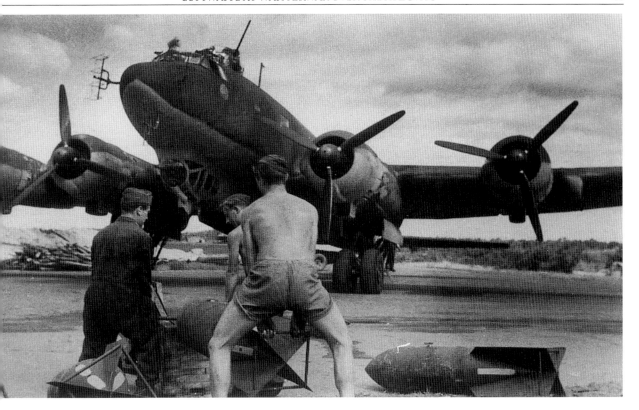

**bove:** Members of the ground crew attempt to transport a SC 250 bomb to their combat aircraft, another of the C-4 series. he C-4, an improved C-3/U5, was capable of carrying out armed reconnaissance missions over great distances as well as nti-shipping duties using aerial torpedoes. Normally only a limited number of bombs were stored in the bomb bay of the -4 to give the aircraft greater endurance over the sea.

**elow:** Fw 200C-4s at Vaernes in Norway stand ready for armed reconnaissance over the North Atlantic and Arctic Oceans. rom mid-1941, these aircraft were increasingly intercepted by Allied long-range aircraft - Liberators, Sunderlands etc., ngaging in a battle of the giants.

**pposite page, top:** A Condor C-4 about to take off from aernes. Even with visibility in excess of 30 miles (50km), it as often the case that no targets were found.

**pposite page, bottom:** This out-of-the-ordinary view shows e upper surfaces of a Fw 200 C-3. Note the MG 131 gun osition on the fuselage. It is possible that this aircraft was ne of the first of some forty long-range armed reconnaissance and combat aircraft produced by Focke-Wulf. The otted lines on the wings mark "no step" areas.

**bove:** This Fw 200 C, possibly rebuilt from a former narmed transport aircraft, has had MG 131 turrets installed on the fuselage roof. KG 40 used aircraft like this for urgent transport duties or the ferrying of ground crews to other bases. Note the windows on the fuselage side, only two of which remain unblanked out.

**Below:** During the disaster of Stalingrad in the winter of 1942-43, a limited number of Fw 200 Cs were pressed into service from flying schools as well as KG 40 in order to increase the air transport capacity of the Luftwaffe. About this time it mounted a desperate attempt to deliver necessary supplies and material to the German 6th Army in and around the city, besieged as it was by massive Russian ground forces.

**Above:** During these missions to support Stalingrad, nine Fw 200 Cs failed to return or were heavily damaged by Soviet AA-fire. Taking off and landing in unfavourable conditions of ice and snow took great skill from pilots engaged in this task. A few of the Fw 200 Cs sent to Stalingrad were captured by Russian forces and were later used by the Soviet Air Force.

**Below:** F8+DL, a Fw 200 C-3, had arrived on the Russian Front late in 1942. On 24 January 1943, only five Fw 200 Cs remained usable for further transport duties due to several technical failures. Only a few days later the German forces surrendered to the encircling Red Army. The remaining Fw 200 Cs returned to Germany to be repaired for further duties.

**Opposite page, top:** Missions were started from Vaernes in Norway during 1942. The four men shown in the photo, taken on 26 July 1944, belong to a crew of five or six and can be seen wearing their full summer flying suits and life jackets. They are listening to a report given by the chief of the ground crew, an NCO who stands before the left engine nacelle. Note the fittings for additional fuel tanks under the wings.

**Opposite page, bottom:** Besides the Fw 200 "Condor", *Kampfgeschwader* 40 also used the He 177 A-3 and A-5. Compared with other combat aircraft, the four-engined Heinkel 177 displayed better operational performance and could carry a higher offensive payload. Note the small KG 4 emblem under the cockpit.

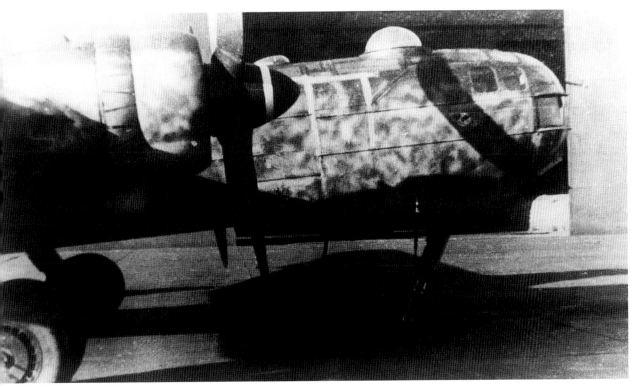

**Above:** The introduction of the He 177 A-3, which was equipped with remote-controlled missiles (mainly the Hs 293 A-1), allowed attacks on enemy merchant ships from greater distances than before. Using these kinds of weapon the crews were not forced to cross the path of the target vessel thus minimising the chance of hits from AA-gunfire.

**Below:** This photo was taken during an exercise held by crews of the fourth and fifth *Staffeln* of KG 40 at Bordeaux-Merignac, a large, well-equipped Luftwaffe airfield situated in southwest France. The first phase of changing their Fw 200 C-3s and C-4s for the He 177 A-5s had just been completed. Note that no Hs 293 A-1 missiles have yet been loaded.

**Opposite page, bottom:** Another view taken on the same day, with at least four He 177 A-5s being seen. Note the first aircraft's port engines have been run up and tested, supervised by a leading member of the ground crew, just prior to takin off. Constant training missions were undertaken using simulated attacks with these aircraft.

**Right:** A fine view of a He 177 A-5, showing the production number 550 043 on the forward fuselage section of this large, well camouflaged combat aircraft. This He 177 (6N+HM) belonged to 4./KG 100 and was heard from for the last time on 9 October 1944. The camouflage seen here was especially developed for anti-shipping raids over the Mediterranean Sea and the Atlantic Ocean.

**Above:** This He 177 A-5 with the production number 550 030 was photographed early in 1944, and also belonged to the fourth *Staffel* of KG 100. When used in low-level attacks on maritime targets, the MG 151/20 fixed in the lower part of the forward cockpit had shown itself to be a dangerous weapon against unarmoured targets. At this time in the war fuel was already limited, so everything was done to save fuel. Note the horse drawn vehicle behind the bomber.

**Opposite page:** This He 177 A-5 (production number 550 077) belonged to the fifth *Staffel* of KG 100 and shows the tactical code 6N+AN. The rear gunner of this He 177 succeeded in shooting down an American Black Widow heavy night fighter over France. The crew were accompanied by their *Schäferhund* (sheepdog) during most of their combat missions in 1944.

**Below:** These He 177 A-5s are being loaded with Hs 293 A-1 remote-controlled bombs in June 1944 and are almost ready for take-off from Bordeaux-Merignac. More than fifteen He 177 A-5s can be seen in this picture, moving to take-off position from two directions. The number of aircraft seen here appears high for German operational strength, but even so, only a few successful hits were reported with the Hs 293 A-1s due to technical failures.

**Above:** Several of the heavy four-engined He 177 A-5s were damaged without any enemy action due to engine or hydraulic failures. Because of the close proximity of the outer metal skin of the wings to the DB 610-engines, hot oil lost from the engines' pistons could often burn through the aircraft's skin, leading to total loss during long-range missions or when transferring to other operational bases.

**Below:** This He 177 A-5 was captured at a destroyed hangar at Châteaudun in France as Allied forces advanced through France during the second half of 1944. One other Heinkel aircraft was maintained in this huge hangar, but such tasks came to an abrupt end shortly before Allied soldiers appeared. Some of the parts, e.g. propellers, have been taken away and used for other aircraft in the unit.

**Above:** The German bomber force based in France from 1940 onward was first engaged in attacking British targets. Subsequently, the destruction of maritime vessels became more urgent, but due to the limited number of German maritime aircraft only a few successes were initially achieved. To counteract the overwhelming number of Allied heavy fighters then appearing in theatre, KG 40 received its own destroyer formation equipped with Ju 88 Cs.

**Right:** A destroyer crew entering their Ju 88 C-6 of 13./KG 40 using the hatch beneath the cockpit section. These aircraft were often fitted with one or two large 600-litre drop tanks mounted under the inner sections of both wings. A total of three MG FF/M and an additional three fixed MG 17s were installed in the forward section of these destroyers.

**Above:** One of the Ju 88 C-6s lost in an attack on Lorient on 23 September 1944 was this aircraft, having the production number 0381 and belonging to 13./KG 40. The aircraft (F8+BY) was camouflaged in a standard splinter scheme over all upper surfaces and featured a white or yellow ring around both propeller spinners.

**Below:** The Ju 88 destroyer aircraft used by KG 40 also carried out close protection of German submarines. These vessels heading to and from their bases often became victims of British Coastal Command aircraft whose crews tried to destroy those U-boats coming within range of American and British Liberator bombers. RAF Sunderland flying boats were also active in this role.

**Above:** On 9 November 1943, the German submarine U 515 is greeted by a Ju 88 destroyer belonging to I./ZG 1, formerly IV./KG 40. Despite having their own AA capability, German submarines were often hit during Anti-Submarine Warfare (ASW) missions, sometimes being unable to dive again. After British Coastal Command sent Mosquito fighters to intercept the submarines the chances of the Ju 88 C, commanded by *Hauptmann* Horst Grahl, providing a suitable U-boat escort were severely reduced.

**Right:** With time, the camouflage of the Ju 88 C-6s was altered. Instead of the green splinter camouflage, grey schemes were increasingly used. As well as its Ju 88 C-6s, I./ZG 1, which was established from parts of IV./KG 40 on 13 October 1943, used the Ju 88 R-2, differing from the C-6 in its use of BMW 801 radial engines. This photo was taken from inside the cockpit of one of these aircraft and shows the fixed armament fitted alongside the pilot's position.

**Above:** A close formation of Ju 88 C-6s belonging to the 14th *Staffel* of KG 40 flying to intercept aircraft belonging to British Coastal Command. During missions such as this, V./KG 1 (and I./ZG 1) suffered several losses. Besides more than 220 men missing or killed in action, 58 were killed in accidents together with 51 men wounded. The unit lost a total of 88 aircraft in action and a further 26 in accidents.

**Below:** Only a few Ju 88 G-1s found their way to I./ZG 1. One of these belonged to the 3rd *Staffel* of ZG 1. On 7 June 1944, this aircraft, commanded by *Unteroffizier* Kurt Strobel, was pronounced missing in action along with its entire crew. The aircraft differed from the C-6 and R-2 by its large antennae situated in front of the fuselage.

**Right:** The few Ju 88 A-14s fitted with the FuG 200 *Hohenthwiel* radar installation and used by *Fernaufk-lärungsgruppe* 123 only played a limited role in the war. During the air struggle over France many of these were destroyed or crashed after being hit by Allied fighter action, mostly in the western part of the country. The aircraft shown had survived 100 missions and was armed with an additional MG FF machine gun in the nose.

**Right:** Taken at an aircraft graveyard, this photo shows the same aircraft together with a Ju 88 D-1 used by FAGr. 123. The aircraft was formerly used by KG 26 which operated the 'plane as a torpedo bomber. The torpedo system can be seen on the right hand side of the fuselage along with the wireless operator's instruments inside the open cockpit.

**Opposite page:** Only ten aircraft (two prototypes and eight series aircraft) of the Ju 88 H-1 variant were produced. The development of this new long-range aircraft started at Dessau early in 1943, with the assistance of the design office of the SNCASO at Chatillon, France and the Junkers bureau in Paris. The picture shows Luftwaffe officers of *Fernaufklärungsgruppe* 123 in France inspecting the first of these aircraft to arrive in early 1944.

**Right:** Under the fuselage of this Ju 88 H-1 can be seen the so-called *Waffentropfen* (weapons drops) with two rearward firing guns mounted, with the small hatch nearby allowing entrance to the cockpit. The first missions of this variant were flown in May 1944. In a mission of over eight hours the crew would cover a distance of about 3,000 km (1,863 miles). On a flight from Rennes, France, via the Lisbon area, the aircraft would turn north of Iceland and then the British Isles before returning to France.

**Below:** This Ju 88 H-1 (DO+FS), photographed on 21 February 1944, was powered by two BMW 801 D-1 radial engines. The fuselage was lengthened before and behind the wing roots, the antennae belonging to the FuG 200 anti-shipping radar fixed on the nose section. At this time the rearward firing armament was yet to be installed or had been removed.

**Above:** The BV 222 flying boats were the largest operational aircraft of the German Luftwaffe. They were used as a long-range transport as well as a reliable reconnaissance aircraft, often powered by six BMW-Bramo 323 radial engines. The first reconnaissance flying boat, BV 222 V2, was intended to command *Fliegerführer Atlantik* in May 1943, in order to secure closer co-operation with German submarines. The aircraft shown was maintained on the French coast.

**Below:** By the time this photo was taken, the BV 222s were armed with heavy machine guns. They were equipped with a MG 151/20, a cannon positioned in a turret fixed over the forward fuselage, which helped to secure the flying boat against attacking carrier-borne fighters or heavy land-based fighter aircraft. After operating under the *Lufttransportstaffel* (LTS) 222 between May 1941 and October 1942, all remaining BV 222s came under the command of *Fliegerführer Atlantik*.

**Above:** Only eight BV 222s survived to the second half of 1944. Most of these had been operating from bases in Norway to control the Southern Arctic and the maritime regions over Iceland and the Northern Atlantic. Besides those few captured in Norway, two others were found by British troops at Travemünde, three BV 222s being sent to England and the USA for further evaluation in the summer of 1945.

**Below:** The Blohm & Voss BV 238 was a giant of a flying boat powered by six DB 603 piston engines, only one ever being completed. Due to the progress of the war, Blohm & Voss was unable to finish the second one. It was suggested that four experimental aircraft (BV 238 V1 to V4) be built, followed by 25 production aircraft, these to be made from October 1942 to December 1945. However, the first experimental aircraft took off for the first time no earlier than 10 March 1944.

After the disastrous air raids against the city of Hamburg and the destruction of the Wenzendorf works of Blohm & Voss, it was decided to hide the massive BV 238 on the shores of the Schaalsee near Lübeck. Since it was impossible to find suitable camouflage for the aircraft, it was discovered by enemy fighters and destroyed by strafing Mustangs on 4 May 1945. The aircraft never flew an operational mission.

**Above:** Seen in 1944, this Ju 290 A-5 used by the *Fernaufklärungsgruppe* 5 shows the emblem of the second *Staffel* of that long-range reconnaissance unit. A single MG 151/20 machine gun could be installed on both forward weapon positions. The antennae seen here are part of the FuG 200 radar system. The camouflage layout shows the operational nature of this four-engined aircraft.

**Right:** After shutting off the engines, a member of the ground crew cleans the large propeller blades of this Ju 290 A-5 of *FAGr.* 5, prior to its next maritime operation. Operational from October 1943, *FAGr.* 5 was disbanded in August 1944.

**Opposite page, top:** This Ju 290 A-5 (KR+LA, production number 110170), possibly also designated as experimental Ju 290 V6, was the first of eleven A-5s. After being tested at Rechlin, it was handed over to FAGr. 5 but withdrawn in August 1944. The aircraft, formerly 9V+DH, then became an experimental airframe fitted with one HeS 11 turbine. It was destroyed early in 1945 during an air raid.

**Opposite page, bottom:** The armament of the first Ju 290 A-5 consisted of two MG 151/20s fitted on the fuselage roof. Two more MG 151/20 cannon were mounted in beam positions in the front and rear sections of the fuselage. In the bulge under the cockpit section a single MG 131 was used for defensive purposes, whilst in the rear fuselage it was possible to install two more MG 151/20 guns.

**Top right:** This shows a very rare shot taken during one of many dangerous missions over the stormy Atlantic Ocean in 1943 or 1944. Two Ju 290s, an A-5 and an A-7, head for their target far from the French coastline. Due to bad weather and the Allied capacity for using escort carriers with well-protected convoys, the number of available combat crews became fewer and fewer.

**Bottom right:** This Ju 290 A-7 (9V+GK, formerly KR+LL, production number 110181) was handed over to *Fernaufklärungsgruppe* 5 and first flown on 2 May 1944 , where it was used by *Leutnant* Ernst and his crew. The aircraft had belonged to the second *Staffel* of *Fernaufklärungsgruppe* 5. From August 1944 it was used by crews of 1./KG 200 before being destroyed by bombs at Dessau on 16 August 1944.

**Left:** This shot of the twin-wheeled undercarriage of the Ju 290 shows the large proportions of this four-engined long-range aircraft. The crewmember of *Fernaufklärungsgruppe* 5 shown, an NCO, was decorated with the *Eisernes Kreuz* (Iron Cross) first class and his insignia show him to be a pilot.

**Below:** This Ju 290 A-5 (KR+LK, production number 110180) was flown for the first time on 23 March 1944 by Junkers pilot Dautzenberg. The aircraft was then handed over to 1./*Fernaufklärungsgruppe* 5 on 10 August 1944 where it received the tactical code 9V+KH. The aircraft was subsequently transferred to Rechlin-Roggentin where it was destroyed on 10 April 1945 during an air raid.

**Right:** This mock-up of the nose section of a Ju 290 A-7 long-range reconnaissance aircraft shows the installation of a movable MG 151/20 gun. Thirteen of the twenty aircraft ordered were ready by the summer of 1944. The aircraft were fitted with FuG 200 radar and could be used with remote-controlled bombs mounted under both ETC 200 racks. Subsequently a FuG 203e wireless operation system was added.

**Below:** In an attempt to achieve even greater flight endurance, Junkers began construction of the Ju 390 A-1. Instead of four BMW 801 Ds, this long-range aircraft was propelled by six BMW 801 E engines. After two experimental aircraft had been completed, all further attempts to enter series production for the type were stopped in 1944 due to the course of the war. A crew of ten to twelve men were to be housed in the fuselage of this large aircraft.

**Left:** Junkers development bureaux calculated that defensive armament consisting of two gun positions each comprising four MG 131s, with a double MG 131 under the forward fuselage and two twin MG 151/20 weapon positions, would be sufficient to protect the Ju 390 A-1 especially if this long-range aircraft were flown in close formation. Series production of the huge Ju 390 was not started due to the lack of both materials and fuel.

**Below:** The last anti-shipping aircraft proposed for missions over the sea, the Ju 388 M-1, was developed for both the anti-shipping and armed reconnaissance roles. Only a limited number of this fast three-seat combat aircraft were produced since the entire development project was terminated in early February 1945. Development of the twin-fuselage version of the Do 335, called the He 635, also ended sooner than anticipated early in 1945.

**Above:** This He 111 belonged to the inventory of KG 26 *Löwengeschwader* and was used as a torpedo bomber carrying two F5 torpedoes from its base in Norway in 1942. The unit was under the command of *Luftflotte* 5.

**Below:** This photo gives an impression of the He 111 H-5/torp. armed with two F5 torpedoes, a type that was widely used by the crews of *Kampfgeschwader* 26.

**Above:** Both F5 torpedoes hung beneath the fuselage of the HE 111 H's could be mounted beneath either a PVC 1006B- or ETC 2000 bomb release system. Due to the performance of the HE 111 bomber, low-level attacks on Allied vessels became very dangerous for all aircrews using this aircraft.

**Below:** Since the take-off weight of the Ju 88 A-4/torp. was so high when carrying two F5 torpedoes, several aircraft were equipped with so called *Krafteiern* (power eggs), small rocket-assisted take-off units fitted under the outer part of both wings. These rocket pods were jettisoned after use, small parachutes carrying them to the ground so that they could be recovered later.

**Opposite page:** After the German aircraft industry started delivery of the Ju 88 A-4/torp. combat aeroplanes in 1943, many He 111 Hs of KG 26 were handed over to other front line units. The aircraft shown is most likely part of III./KG 26, which was one of the first units to receive the new Junkers torpedo bomber.

**Opposite page, top:** In 1944, the inventory of KG 26 changed again after the Ju 88 A-4 was replaced, first by the Ju 88 A-17 and later by the Ju 188. Due to their combat role, all of these aircraft were well camouflaged to avoid being spotted from ships when attacking targets over the southern Arctic and northern Atlantic Oceans.

**Above:** Luftwaffe specialists have just prepared this F5 torpedo before it disappears into the bomb bay of a He 115 floatplane. A weapons mechanic is sitting on the torpedo in order to arm the warhead and to adjust the complicated guidance system of the weapon.

**Left:** During attacks aimed at Allied convoys heading for Russia, a limited number of He 115 floatplanes were engaged. The photo shows the loading of a practice torpedo on the pontoon under the bomb bay of this He 115. The markings of the torpedo indicate that the weapon was not fitted with a warhead.

**Above:** To protect heavy vessels of the *Kriegsmarine* against submarine attacks by the Royal Navy, aircraft of the Luft
frequently escorted ships of their sister service. He 115 floatplanes such as that shown often flew under bad weather
conditions far from the coast in order to carry out this important duty.

**Below:** During an exercise this He 115 crew attempt to attack a German freighter using a dummy F5 torpedo (the warhead
having been removed). Note the disruptive camouflage pattern of the German vessel and the tactics of the aircraft, which is
turning away seconds after the torpedo was released.